WHO WANTS TO BE A

MILLIONAIRE

WHO WANTS TO BE A

MILLIONAIRE

Foreword by Michael P. Davies,
Executive Producer

Essay by David Fisher

CADER BOOKS

Cover and Book Design by Charles Kreloff

ISBN: 0-7868-8577-7

FIRST EDITION

10 9 8 7 6 5 4

· CONTENTS ·

◄ FOREWORD ►

Producing *Who Wants to Be a Millionaire* is the experience of a lifetime. It's not a very glamorous job. I've had those before. I've been in the control room for the Academy Awards, counting down with the second hand ready to go live to a billion people worldwide. I've done thousands of hours of television. I should be cynical by now. But this job is the most exciting I've had by far, despite the grueling behind-the-scenes life. During the one week of prep and the two weeks we're on the air live at the studio, I hardly sleep (we have to edit the program overnight to deliver it to ABC the next afternoon), I'm too nervous to eat and, as the chairman of ABC told me when he visited me at work, I look awful. But I wouldn't swap it for any job in the world; it's what my whole career has prepared me for, and it's the only thing I have wanted to do since I first saw the British version of the program in September of 1998. There are four reasons why:

• It's a perfect show. That has nothing to do with me but everything to do with a team of people in Britain who created the show and turned it into what I believe is the greatest quiz show format of all time.

• The second reason is my staff. I love them all—Regis, the producers, the associate producers, the production assistants, the director and crew, the editors, even our runners Dennis and Jaret.

• Then come the contestants. I just flat out care about these people and am astounded by their range of knowledge. You might think the show looks easy but I defy you to get up there in that hot seat, under the lights, with that music and have the composure and courage in your knowledge to keep on going. Qualifying isn't a breeze, either; it's tough to make it onto the show and tough to make it through the fastest-finger round and into the hot seat (the chair in which contestants sit).

• Finally, and I thought cynical television producers were not meant to feel like this, but I love the fact that viewers love it (and I cannot tell you how happy I am that you love the show enough to buy this book). People don't just watch *Millionaire*, or simply like it, they love it. We've heard so many great stories—sports bars with every TV tuned to our show, treadmills stationary at gyms all over the country with motionless runners and walkers captivated by our program, young people, old people, all kinds of people throwing parties to watch us, couples rearranging schedules to make sure they don't miss a second. And most gratifying of all, families, for the first time in memory, watching the same show, in the same room, all totally involved and together.

People always ask me why I think this show works. Like everyone else, I have my theories. Monty Hall once told me that every great game show has one moment where the contestant will either win everything or lose everything. Our show has that moment again and again and everything— the lighting, the music, the direction, even Regis—works to raise the tension of those moments to the highest degree.

Plus, Regis is superb. We had a great role model in Chris Tarrant, the extremely talented broadcaster who hosts the show in Britain. And Regis totally gets it. He understands the moments; he appeals to everyone; he takes these contestants who we've never met, who are extremely nervous, who might not have the most TV-ready personalities, and gives us gold. Who can forget the exchange when one contestant awaiting the verdict on his answer exclaimed, "I'm a fat man, Regis, my heart can't take it!" and Regis calmly responded, "I'm just trying to help you sweat off a few pounds!"

Another key is that the questions on our show are not typical game show questions. They stay up on the screen a long time, they are multiple choice, they are interesting, and they seem easy. The truth is, they're not. But the fact that everyone at home thinks they can do better is vital to the success of the program. To win on this show you need a staggering range of knowledge. Unlike *Jeopardy* or other quiz shows, you can't decide to skip a question or take a guess, get it wrong, lose a few dollars and keep going. You have to be sure on this show and you must be right every time. The consequences of taking a risk and giving a wrong answer are massive. The questions are designed so there is always a large part of the audience screaming at the TV screen, but we all have gaps in our knowledge and when you're steaming along, almost inevitably, a question comes up that will stop you in your tracks. Contestant Michael Shutterly might have been able to correctly identify every twentieth-century pope by his real name but there was no way he was going to know, for sure, that Jethro Tull won the first-ever Grammy for Hard Rock/Metal. I'd love to meet someone who would have known the answers to both. Our contestants earn their dough. Believe me, it is high pressure out there. In fact, our contestants are more than contestants, they're stars. I credit Chris Tarrant for pointing this out to me, but in a lot of ways *Millionaire* is like a real-people soap opera.

Finally, contrary to what everyone in the television business was saying before this summer, there is a place in prime time for the quiz show. In fact, I would go as far as to say it is the birthright of the genre. American television was founded on all kinds of live television: the quiz show, the panel show, the variety show, all what we would now call "alternative" series. There is nothing alternative about *Millionaire*. It is steeped in the tradition of 1950s prime-time television. Yes, it is a precursor to the future, when programing will be a medium that merges television, the computer, and the telephone. But this show is also a throwback, a tip of the hat, a tribute to the great men and women who left theater and radio to build this magnificent and magical thing called television in the 1950s. Joe Cates understands, he was there watching over us. Right, Gil?

I've lost you all, and I'm sorry. Joe Cates was one of the greatest television producers of all time, and his brother Gil still is. So this book is for them, and for all of you who love this program and want to see how you measure up. Maybe, if you get really good, I'll see you at the show. I can't promise you a million dollars, but I do promise that if you make it into the hot seat, for one night, or maybe two, people all over America will be screaming at you on the television and talking about you the next day.

—Michael P. Davies
Executive Producer, *Who Wants to Be a Millionaire*

HOW TO BE A MILLIONAIRE

"This could be it," Regis Philbin said, smiling broadly, *"this could be it. One million dollars. You've won a half million, going for a million."*

This was the ninth night Who Wants to Be a Millionaire *was broadcast. Sitting opposite Regis in the hot seat was Michael Shutterly, an attorney and boy scout leader from Richmond, Virginia, who had successfully selected the correct name of Pope John Paul I from four possibilities to win $500,000. "We're all terribly excited for Michael Shutterly," Regis continued, holding up a check for a half million dollars. "He has just won the biggest prize in prime-time television history."*

Regis explained the situation carefully. Shutterly had used all three lifelines: he'd phoned a friend, asked the audience, and gone 50:50. According to the rules, even after hearing the question he could choose to take his winnings and leave, but once he gave his final answer he would lose $468,000 if he was wrong, leaving with only $32,000.

But if…if Shutterly answered one more question correctly, just one more, he would become the first person in television history to win a million dollars.

Shutterly was calm as Regis read the million dollar question, "On February 22, 1989, what group won the first Grammy for Best Hard Rock/Metal Performance? Was it Metallica? AC/DC? Living Colour? Jethro Tull?"

The studio was absolutely silent. Did he know the

answer? If not, was it worth risking $468,000 to win $1,000,000? In the control room Executive Producer Michael Davies was silently rooting for Shutterly. The camera focused on Shutterly's wife, who had a proud smile frozen on her face. Shutterly sat silently, thinking...thinking...

Finally, he smiled wryly, "One difficulty is there's only one of the four I've ever listened to," he explained calmly, "and it's definitely not them." He smiled contentedly, "I will not be a millionaire. I'll be half a millionaire."

"Is that your final decision?" Regis asked.

Shutterly nodded, "Yes, it is." The audience exploded into cheers. Regis nodded in acceptance. Then he handed Michael Shutterly the largest one-time cash prize (excluding lotteries) in the history of American television.

There was no question about it, the night *Who Wants to Be a Millionaire* went on the air for the first time on August 16, 1999, the world of television was changed forever. The show broke all the long-accepted rules: it was a quiz show broadcast in prime time on thirteen of fourteen consecutive nights; it was being introduced in the midst of the summer viewing doldrums and offered contestants the chance to win up to $1,000,000; it was based on a British program, the rules of which had been changed only slightly; contestants had absolutely no time limit in which to answer the questions and were encouraged to seek help in answering them—and they even had the option of leaving with their previous winnings *after* seeing the question.

This was potentially the recipe for a legendary broadcasting disaster. It could have cost the ABC network a fortune and survived only as the punchline of endless jokes. Instead, while breaking all the rules, it also broke all the records. It was the most successful new show ever introduced in the summer, the ratings increased just about every single night, it attracted viewers from every demographic group—and it sent rival networks scurrying to develop big-prize quiz shows of their own. *Millionaire* captivated America in just two weeks, and host Regis Philbin's somber question, "Is that your final answer?" became a catchphrase.

• THE DETAILS AND THE DRAMA •

The rules of the game are deceptively simple: To win $1,000,000 a contestant has to correctly answer fifteen multiple-choice questions of increasing difficulty from a broad range of categories. The prize money roughly doubles with each correct answer. Contestants can stop at any time and leave with their winnings, or after seeing the question and four possible answers can decide to stop and still leave with their winnings. If they answer incorrectly but have successfully answered at least the first five questions, they receive a minimum of $1,000; once contestants have correctly answered the $32,000 question, they lock in that amount, even if a subsequent question is answered incorrectly. Players can take as much time as needed to answer a question—one person took eighteen minutes before telling Regis it was his "final answer" (later edited down to six minutes for the broadcast). And contestants all have three lifelines that can be used at any time: they can phone a friend, they can ask the audience, or they can double their odds by requesting two of the four possible answers be eliminated— but each lifeline can be used only once.

What made the show instantly successful, believes

Michael Davies, who brought it over from England and fought to get it on, is the inherent drama. "This show has a perfect three-act dramatic structure. The setup is clear, we know what the contestants want to accomplish, the conflict is incredible as they try to achieve that goal, and no one knows what the resolution will be until the last moment.

"The show works because our contestants are ordinary people suddenly thrust into the spotlight and given a chance to win enough money to change their lives. They don't even know they're going to be on the show until two days before the actual taping. Other quiz shows test their contestants' knowledge—we test the courage of their convictions. *Millionaire* isn't just about how smart they are, it's about how much they are willing to risk. Most of our contestants have to make the biggest financial decision of their lives in front of several million people. At times the suspense is incredible."

• A QUEST FOR THE PERFECT QUIZ •

To bring the show to America, the British-born Davies also had to take a great risk. When he joined Disney in 1992 he was charged by Chairman Michael Eisner with looking for a big money prime-time quiz show. Eisner believed that four decades after the quiz show scandals (in which popular contestants were being given the correct answers to enable them to continue to appear), the time was right for another prime-time quiz show.

Among the first programs Davies tried to develop was a new version of the most popular quiz show in history, *The $64,000 Question*, but Davies just couldn't get it to work to his satisfaction. Meanwhile, he developed two other quiz shows, *Debt* for Lifetime and *Win Ben Stein's Money* for Comedy Central, and defied the common belief that British shows don't work in America by successfully transporting the English comedy game show *Whose Line Is It Anyway?* to ABC in prime time. When he joined the ABC network in 1998 he became a program buyer, still looking for a prime-time quiz show.

Meanwhile, a small English production company, Celador, was developing a prime-time quiz show entitled *Cash Mountain* in which contestants qualified to be on the show by answering a computer-run telephone quiz, had lifelines to help them if they got on the show, and could quit and keep their winnings after seeing a question if not positive about the answer. During three years in development the show became *Who Wants to Be a Millionaire.*

Davies heard about the excitement surrounding the show the day before Britain's ITV broadcast it for the first time. As soon as he acquired a tape to watch, he remembers that, "I was completely blown away. I knew a few things instantly. First, this was the prime-time show Michael Eisner had been looking for. Second, I thought it was the best quiz show format and perhaps the best nonfiction television format I'd seen in my life. Third, I knew I wanted to leave my job and produce it. And finally, I knew there would be a phenomenal bidding war for the American rights to the show and it was going to be incredibly difficult to obtain them."

Davies was right. *Who Wants to Be a Millionaire* captivated Britain. It became one of the most watched programs in British TV history and television networks from countries around the world began trying to license the rights.

• SECURING THE RIGHTS •

Davies showed the tape to executives at ABC. While they also loved it, they questioned if it would work in the United States. They wanted to do a pilot, a test show. "I knew a pilot wouldn't work," Davies recalls, "because we weren't going to really be giving away a million dollars. People wouldn't be playing for real. There would be no dramatic tension as they had nothing to lose." Davies then took two huge gambles: he guaranteed creator Paul Smith that he would get the show scheduled in prime time on consecutive nights exactly as it had first been aired in Britain—even though he had absolutely no assurance of that from ABC—and he gave notice to the network that he would leave his job to produce it.

The key to selling the concept Davies had promised became finding an acceptable host. Davies put together a wish list of candidates, among them Bob Costas, Phil Donahue, Montel Williams...and Regis Philbin. When Davies had been trying to develop *$64,000 Question*, Philbin had been his first choice to host it. "Regis is rooted in what I love about broadcasting. He has the rare ability to make spontaneity seem well produced. I've always felt he was ageless, he appeals to people of all ages, while still retaining an edge."

Coincidentally, Regis Philbin had also obtained a tape of the British broadcast and called Davies. "I don't know if you're interested in me," he said, "but there is nothing I've ever wanted to do in my career as much as I want to do this show. I'll audition, I'll do a pilot, I'll go with you to London, but I want to do it." During that long conversation everything he said convinced Davies that Philbin understood the format and why it was so appealing to viewers. Davies hung up the phone and retyped his wish list. At the top was Regis Philbin, underlined for emphasis. From that moment on, Davies had no doubt Philbin would host the show.

And it has become clear that Regis is the perfect host. Davies describes him as "a fire starter," meaning he has the rare ability to draw meaningful answers from people he's met for only a few minutes. One contestant confided in front of millions of people that he and his wife had been "trying unsuccessfully to get pregnant, so we're going to use our winnings to adopt a baby."

Once Regis agreed to host the show, ABC nervously agreed to broadcast the show on consecutive nights in prime time in August. It was that commitment, Davies believes, that transformed *Who Wants to Be a Millionaire* from a quiz show into an event. "If we were scheduled once weekly we would have been perceived as just another new show," he explains, "but this decision got the media writing about the show, it made the viewing audience curious to see what we were all about." With ABC's commitment and the extensive power of the Disney organization behind him, Davies was finally able to secure the American broadcasting rights. Now all he had to do was make television history.

• PICKING THE CONTESTANTS •

From the way contestants were found to the way the game was played, there had never been a program like *Who Wants to Be a Millionaire* in this country. The process of selecting contestants for the initial thirteen broadcasts began with an ad asking viewers "Who wants to be a millionaire?" and informing them that by calling a 900-number (some states required 800-numbers), answering three questions correctly in the fastest time, and being the top scorers in a playoff game, they could be on their way to New York City. The cost of the call was $1.50, and callers were restricted to two calls from the same phone each day. Revenues from these phone calls were to be used to defer the costs of producing the show.

In Britain this technique had been tremendously successful, but initially here there were substantially fewer calls than expected. "Calling a 900-number can have a real taboo about it," explains Supervising Producer Ann Miller, "and so many people have 900-blocks on their phones to prevent their kids from using it." (Callers now use a free 800-number to qualify.)

Players were asked to answer three general-knowledge questions increasing in difficulty. Each question required players to put four things in the proper order using their telephone keypad. One question, for example, told players to "put the following cities in order from east to west, traveling along Route 66: Albuquerque, Tulsa, Amarillo, Beverly Hills." Players who answered all the questions correctly were ranked on speed of response. About 7 percent of callers answered all three questions correctly. These players were then asked to select one of the available thirteen tape dates for which they wanted to qualify. (If you try calling in, Davies advises that you, "prepare yourself with a pen, paper, and chart for the answers *before* you make the phone call.")

There was a playoff for each tape date, held among the top scorers from each day who selected the same tape date. The playoff consisted of five questions of increasing difficulty, answered by placing the items in the correct order. Again, players who answered all the questions correctly were ranked based on the speed of their responses.

• WELCOME TO THE SHOW •

The contestant department received the results within thirty minutes of the completion of each playoff game and had from 7:30 P.M. to 9:00 P.M. to notify and qualify the winning players and arrange for them and a friend to come to New York the next day. Doing it that way can be a logistical nightmare, but it gives the show an immediacy not found on any other game show. The top ten scorers were qualified as finalists and the next two highest-scorers were qualified as alternates. All won a trip to New York and the finalists had the opportunity to compete on-air to play the game. The moment they arrived in New York was the first time any member of the show staff met with the contestants. The contestants didn't make it on the show because of how they looked or their personalities. They made it because of their ability to answer general-knowledge questions rapidly. The contestants for the first thirteen programs came in all sizes and shapes, they were young and old, they came from all over the country, they did all kinds of jobs and were married and single. In short, they were representative of ordinary Americans. The most surprising thing about this group of players was that it consisted of many more men than women. Although no one is quite sure why, Ann Miller suggests that judging by speed favored people used to playing video games—mostly men. Speed of response has been eliminated in the first telephone qualifying round for upcoming series of contests. The rest of the process has been kept much the same.

Once at the hotel they receive packets of information about the show and meet with show staff to go over their schedules. About the only preparation for the broadcast they're given are instructions not to wear clothes with small checked prints, very bright colors or corporate logos.

They arrive at the studio at about noon the day of the taping, and once in the studio are never out of the sight of the contestant department's staff. During the day they're interviewed so Regis will have some basic information to use when he talks with them, they're shown episodes of the program and the rules of the game are reviewed. Finally, they are taken into the studio where Michael Davies greets them and tells them what's going to happen. Then they are seated in the same seats in which they will be during the show and, under broadcast conditions—the same lighting and the same cues—they rehearse playing the "fastest-finger game."

The contestants who actually get to sit in the hot seat do so by winning the fastest-finger competition—answering one question in the shortest period of time—on the air. When the contestants feel comfortable with the mechanics of the fastest-finger game, Regis joins them and they rehearse with a special set of sample questions. Each person has to come and sit in the hot seat. Actually, getting into the chair is a little tricky. It swivels and tips, so people have to get used to it. Once in the chair, facing Regis, each contestant tries out the three lifelines: members of the crew play the audience and someone in the control room plays the phone-friend. Contestants are encouraged not to be shy about explaining their answer selections, but it's incumbent on Regis to draw them out as well. The object is to get the contestant used to playing the game under the glare of hot lights, and hearing Regis ask, "Is that your final answer?"

It's very important that contestants understand that Regis *wants* them to win the big prize. He reassures them that he is not trying to trick them or convince them to change their answer, and he is not there to intimidate them or speed them up. As host, Regis has to walk a fine line between squeezing all the possible tension out of a moment and not influencing a contestant to either commit to one answer or change his mind. In fact, Regis is not given the answer to any questions until the contestant has confirmed that it is his or her final answer and the response is locked into the computer.

• THOSE QUESTIONS •

The questions contestants will be asked have been prepared weeks in advance and stored securely in a computer data-base. Ten people working in Los Angeles have written the questions under Coordinating Producer Terrence McDonnell and Miller's supervision. After a question is written a researcher confirms from the source material—books, ency-clopedias, almanacs, the Internet, newspapers, magazines, and just about anywhere else—that the answer is correct, then backs it up with two additional sources. Then researchers do a negative search to make sure that none of the three other selections could also be correct.

Questions are grouped in stacks of fifteen questions— the ladder to $1,000,000. The actual stacks to be used in each show are selected daily at random by ABC's Broadcast Standards and Practices representative. The challenge is to create a stack that covers an incredibly broad range of knowledge, everything from the names of the Spice Girls to the current president of South Africa. The best questions for the show aren't necessarily very difficult, they're ques-tions the contestant knows they once knew or should know, and questions that viewers also can answer. A good question, for example, would be, "How many red stripes are currently on the 50-star U.S. flag: Five, Six, Seven or

Eight?" That's the type of question to which people know the answer, they think. It's um...or is it...? (It's seven.)

Surprisingly, the easiest questions are the most difficult to write. "By the time a person is sitting in the hot seat, he or she has gone through the phone game, come to New York, gone through the rehearsal and won the fastest-finger game," explains Miller. "The contestant sits down under the hot lights, facing Regis, and suddenly 200 people in the studio audience are staring at them, the heartbeat music is playing and they remember that there is $1,000,000 at stake. In that position some people can't even remember their own name. So the first few questions are easy, just to give the contestant a chance to relax."

But even some easy questions can be hard to answer. One early question asked, "Who played the title role in *Rainman*?" Originally both Dustin Hoffman and Tom Cruise were among the choices, but just to make it easier Miller eliminated Cruise. The next day, she recalls, she had numerous phone calls incorrectly asking her why nobody had noticed they accepted the wrong answer: Dustin Hoffman. (Hoffman's character was named Raymond; Cruise's character, Raymond's younger brother, called him Rainman as a young boy.)

But even with all the checking and double-checking, *Who Wants to Be a Millionaire* made news headlines during its initial run by declaring the right answer wrong. The question was, "Which of these Great Lakes is largest by area?" While Lake Superior is the largest of the Great Lakes it was not one of the choices, making the correct answer to the question Lake Huron. For Regis's information the question researcher had noted that, "if the contestant picks Lake Michigan, it is the largest by volume," but then made the mistake of checking Lake Michigan as the correct answer rather than Lake Huron. The contestant correctly responded "Lake Huron," to which Regis told him he was incorrect.

When the taping was over the other contestants immediately informed Ann Miller that the show's answer was wrong. Within minutes she had confirmed that the contestant was correct and he was invited by Davies to return on the final broadcast. And rather than trying to hide the mistake, Davies ran the tape and announced that an error had been made. The result was a tremendous amount of publicity for the brand new show. "Half my friends claimed we'd made the mistake on purpose," Davies explains, "but if we had, we never could have pulled it off as well."

Because contestants can take as long as they want before answering a question, there is no way to keep the show to the half hour or hour it runs on TV. So as soon as the taping ends, Davies and his staff go into the control booth to edit the show to broadcast length to be run the following night. Only portions of the program not affecting the outcome of the game are edited out. They practically live in the studio, insulated from the outside world, grabbing meals and sleep whenever possible. Making it all come together requires tremendous teamwork and leadership. At the beginning of the show's initial run the staff handed Davies a military helmet and began calling him "Patton."

• MAKING THE MOST OF •
THE LIFELINES

As Davies had predicted, the audience loved watching people just like themselves having to decide whether to risk a small fortune to win a larger fortune. In addition to knowledge, playing the game requires self-confidence and the ability to decide when to use the three lifelines. There is a great deal of strategy involved in that decision. (When the show was originally being conceived many different lifelines were considered, among them having a panel of experts to consult, a single friend in continuous contact by phone, even the opportunity to change the question.)

As the first questions tend to be broad-based general knowledge, contestants usually ask the audience in the early rounds, since the audience comprises a cross-section of ordinary people. A very high percentage of the audience correctly answers questions at the lower levels. For example, 87 percent of the audience knew that most episodes of *Magnum P.I.* took place in Hawaii. One $32,000 question on which the contestant should have relied on the audience was, "What is the only current U.S. coin with a president's profile facing to the right? Half dollar, quarter, nickel, penny." The contestant didn't seem to notice members of the audience taking change out of their pockets and looking at it. By a huge percentage the audience said it was the penny. But he still wasn't sure. He decided to use a second lifeline, and he phoned a friend.

Contestants are allowed to select five friends whom they can telephone for assistance. They are advised to name people who are knowledgeable on different subjects, from which of the Teletubbies is purple to what is seven to the tenth power. Phone-friends are told that if they don't know the answer or aren't positive, they should make sure the contestant knows that, too.

Viewers have written complaining the game must be fixed because the contestant gives Regis just a first name and in one ring the person is on the phone. All of the friends are contacted prior to the show. They're told when to be available, to let the phone ring three times then answer simply, "Hello," and to keep the phone line free between 7 P.M. and 10 P.M. the night of the taping. When a contestant wins the fastest-finger competition and sits in the hot seat, the contestant department calls to tell the five designated people that their friend is playing the game and warns them to be ready. If any of these friends aren't home, the contestant is informed before playing the game. These phone-friends do not stay on hold and they aren't watching the show because it's being taped. And when they are asked for assistance they are only given thirty seconds to respond.

Even phone-friends feel the effects of the pressure. For the question about the coin, the friend could have simply reached into his pocket to examine some coins. But afterwards he explained he was so nervous he didn't think about looking in his pocket. He finally said he thought it was the nickel, but admitted he wasn't sure. The contestant had used two lifelines and gotten two different answers.

The contestant finally used his third and final lifeline, 50:50. This is the only lifeline that is guaranteed to provide helpful information. It eliminates two of the three incorrect answers, doubling the contestant's chances of getting the right answer. If a contestant absolutely doesn't know the answer to a question, 50:50 is probably the best lifeline to use first. Even if that contestant then decides to phone a friend, he's already made it easier for the friend by eliminating two possibilities. Of course, the computer has been programmed to leave the best possible wrong answer. When a contestant was asked, "In Shakespeare's *Romeo and Juliet*, what is Juliet's family name?" she asked for 50:50. The two remaining answers were Capulet and Montague—the wrong answer being Romeo's last name.

As Davies noted, "When there is a substantial sum of money at stake and an even chance of guessing correctly, the tension generated by a contestant deciding whether or not to risk his winnings on a guess is incredible."

When the contestant finally went 50:50 to determine on which coin the president is facing to the right, the choices were the penny and the half dollar. Eighteen minutes after beginning he finally responded, "I'm going to say it's the penny."

When Regis calmly asked, "Is that your final answer?" he nervously nodded his head and said it was—and it was the right answer, securing him $32,000 in winnings. But he had expended his three lifelines, and he missed the following question.

• THE CHECK IS IN YOUR HAND •

When a contestant finally decides to take the money and leave, or their final answer is wrong, Regis hands them a check and they exit. That check is not real, though; six business days after the taping the contestant receives his winnings.

Michael Davies is thrilled with all the checks he gives away and with the success of the show. "I've always believed that, in order to work, nonfiction television programs have to reflect the mood of their age," he said. "*Millionaire* is a complete salute to the great quiz shows of the 1950s, but at the same time I believe it is a precursor to the entertainment platform of the twenty-first century. The days of one person in an isolation booth are long gone, we are in the age of sharing knowledge. It's no longer just a matter of what you know, it's if you know how to find the information you need to know. Eventually the audience will not simply be watching quiz shows, they will be participating in them from their own homes.

"*Millionaire* is the giant next step into the future of television."

• HOW TO PLAY MILLIONAIRE •
AT HOME

In the following pages, you will find a few sample telephone fastest-finger questions and twenty complete *Millionaire* games to test your skill and to play at home with friends. As you play along, don't forget to use your lifelines wisely: phone a friend (or call upon a friend already in the room), ask your audience (even if they're in your living room), and reduce your chances to 50:50. The 50:50 selections for each question can be found one page after the respective question, on the outside of the page underneath the appropriate dollar amount heading. The answers to the questions can be found starting on page 189. Answers are arranged by dollar amount, and listed by the matching game number—so you won't accidentally cast your eyes upon all the answers in the game when you go to check your response.

1. Put the following parts of a horse in order, beginning at the front.

   A. Hind legs
   B. Tail
   C. Muzzle
   D. Withers

2. Place the following performers in the order they joined *Saturday Night Live*, from the earliest to the most recent.

   A. John Belushi
   B. Colin Quinn
   C. Eddie Murphy
   D. Phil Hartman

3. Arrange these famous entrepreneurs in order of their birth, from the oldest to the youngest.

   A. Donald Trump
   B. Bill Gates
   C. Ted Turner
   D. Lee Iacocca

4. Put the following Winter Olmpic host cities in order, from the most recent to the earliest.

A. Innsbruck
B. Lillehammer
C. Nagano
D. Albertville

5. Put the following presidents in the order they appear on Mount Rushmore, from left to right.

A. Jefferson
B. Lincoln
C. Roosevelt
D. Washington

6. Rank the eggs of these animals in order of their standard size, from the smallest to the largest.

A. Hummingbird
B. Mosquito
C. Pheasant
D. Ostrich

ANSWERS
1. CDAB
2. ACDB
3. DCAB
4. CBDA
5. DACB
6. BACD

· GAME 1 ·

$100

According to Emily Post, if a man wants to "cut in" on another couple dancing, what should he do?

A. Take the woman's hand

B. Tap the man's shoulder

C. Tap the woman's shoulder

D. Announce his intention

$200

Which of the following animals does not have antlers?

A. Wapiti

B. White-tailed deer

C. Caribou

D. Beaver

$300

According to the song made popular by singer Tony Bennett, where did he leave his heart?

A. San Diego
B. San Francisco
C. San Bernadino
D. San Luis Obispo

$100

B or D

$500

On the classic television show *Welcome Back Kotter,* which of the following groups was Mr. Kotter assigned to teach?

$200

A or D

A. Sweathogs
B. Greasehogs
C. Bosshogs
D. Filthyhogs

$1,000

On which of the following would you find a clutch lever, twist-grip throttle and pillion footrest?

A. Surrey
B. Rickshaw
C. Ski lift
D. Motorcycle

$300

A or B

$2,000

Which of the following Ben and Jerry's ice cream flavors is named after a music group?

A. Chunky Monkey
B. Wavy Gravy
C. Phish Food
D. Rainforest Crunch

$500

A or B

$4,000

What movie critic wrote the screenplay for Russ Meyer's classic cult movie *Beyond the Valley of the Dolls*?

A. Roger Ebert
B. Gene Siskel
C. Rex Reed
D. Gene Shalit

$1,000

(50:50)

C or D

$8,000

Which of the following football players did not win the Heisman trophy?

$2,000

(50:50)

B or C

A. Ernie Davis
B. O. J. Simpson
C. Jerry Rice
D. Steve Spurrier

$16,000

Which of the following legendary structures was built as a tomb for a queen?

A. Taj Mahal
B. Hagia Sophia
C. Westminster Cathedral
D. Topkapi Palace

$4,000

50:50

A or C

$32,000

Which of the following words is an "eponym"?

A. Leotard
B. Dreidel
C. Splash
D. Xerox

$8,000

50:50

C or D

$64,000

Which of the following is a type of ornamental design found in architecture?

A. Block and tackle
B. Egg and dart
C. Hook and eye
D. Buck and wing

$16,000

A or B

$125,000

What is the name of the flight pattern that NASA uses to achieve weightlessness in Earth's atmosphere?

$32,000

A or D

A. Paramount
B. Parabola
C. Ellipsis
D. Roller coaster

$250,000

Which character in Greek mythology killed his father, married his sister, and ate his own children?

A. Hades
B. Cronos
C. Hephaestus
D. Poseidon

$64,000

50:50

B or C

$500,000

Which of the following passengers did not perish during the sinking of the *Titanic*?

A. J. Bruce Ismay
B. Captain Edward J. Smith
C. Thomas Andrews
D. Benjamin Guggenheim

$125,000

50:50

B or D

$1,000,000

Who has been chosen as the new model for Marianne, the symbol of the French Republic?

A. Laetitia Casta
B. Estelle Hallyday
C. Nathalie Simon
D. Daniela Lumbroso

$250,000

50:50
A or B

$500,000

50:50
A or C

· GAME 2 ·

$100

Which of the following is the term for an investor who anticipates a rise in stock prices?

A. Bear

B. Boar

C. Bull

D. Steer

$200

In the television series *The Six Million Dollar Man*, who did Steve Austin report to?

A. Reuben Kincaid

B. Jim Phelps

C. Oscar Goldman

D. Charlie

$1,000,000

50:50
A or B

$300

During the Persian Gulf War, what color ribbon was popularly used to honor American soldiers?

A. Red
B. Blue
C. Black
D. Yellow

$100

50:50

A or C

$500

In the U.S. music business, when an album "goes platinum," a minimum of how many copies have been sold?

A. 100,000
B. 200,000
C. 500,000
D. 1,000,000

$200

50:50

C or D

$1,000

What magazine did Miramax Films cofound?

A. *People*
B. *TV Guide*
C. *Elle*
D. *Talk*

$300

A or D

$2,000

Which of the following was discovered by Galileo?

A. Moons of Jupiter
B. Ring of Kerry
C. Star of David
D. Laura Palmer

$500

C or D

$4,000

Who of the following has never been related to actor George Clooney?

A. Rosemary Clooney
B. José Ferrer
C. Debby Boone
D. Mark Wahlberg

$1,000

50:50

A or D

$8,000

According to the Bible, what is the moral of "The Prodigal Son" parable?

A. Trust
B. Forgiveness
C. Freedom
D. Justice

$2,000

50:50

A or B

$16,000

In what arithmetic process would you find a minuend and subtrahend?

A. Addition
B. Subtraction
C. Multiplication
D. Division

$4,000

B or D

$32,000

Which of the following cities has never hosted a World's Fair?

A. Seattle, WA
B. Osaka, Japan
C. Toronto, Canada
D. Knoxville, TN

$8,000

A or B

$64,000

The name of which state originates from an Indian word meaning "at the long tidal river"?

A. Connecticut
B. Mississippi
C. California
D. Missouri

$16,000

50:50

B or D

$125,000

Howard University was named after which founding member of the Freedman's Bureau?

$32,000

50:50

A or C

A. J. Imogene Howard
B. General Oliver Howard
C. Howard Taft
D. Edwin Clarence Howard

$250,000

What scale is used to measure the damage caused by an earthquake?

A. Mercalli
B. Saffir-Simpson
C. Humboldt
D. Volcus

$500,000

The words to the song "Hail to the Chief" come from a poem written by which of the following people?

A. Sir Thomas Malory
B. Francis Scott Key
C. Sir Walter Scott
D. James Sanderson

$1,000,000

What was the first company to air a television commercial in the U.S.?

A. Texaco
B. Sweetheart Soap
C. Bulova Company
D. Geritol

$250,000

A or D

$500,000

C or D

· GAME 3 ·

$100

Who started with a single five-and-dime store before going on to found Wal-Mart?

A. Walter Johnson
B. Sam Walton
C. Martin Delany
D. Wally Martin

$200

On most standard American Touch-Tone phones, what button is directly left of "0"?

A. #
B. *
C. 9
D. 1

A or C

$300

In the 1984 movie *Footloose*, which of the following activities is outlawed?

A. Dancing
B. Jogging
C. Walking
D. Spitting

$100

50:50

B or C

$500

What is the proper thing to do with a chorizo?

A. Eat it
B. Drink it
C. Ride it
D. Read it

$200

50:50

A or B

$1,000

As of November 1999, who of the following had never guest-hosted *The Tonight Show*?

A. David Letterman
B. Martin Short
C. Garry Shandling
D. Kermit the Frog

$300

A or D

$2,000

Which author began one of his classic books with the phrase, "It was the best of times, it was the worst of times"?

A. F. Scott Fitzgerald
B. J. R. R. Tolkien
C. Charles Dickens
D. Ernest Hemingway

$500

A or C

$4,000

In which wing of the White House in Washington, D.C. would you find the Oval Office?

A. The East Wing
B. The West Wing
C. The South Wing
D. The North Wing

A or B

$8,000

Which country music star wrote the song "Crazy," made famous by singer Patsy Cline?

A. Kenny Rogers
B. Willie Nelson
C. Merle Haggard
D. George Jones

A or C

$16,000

On what ship did Charles Darwin serve as a naturalist during a five-year voyage in the 1830s?

A. The *Bountiful*
B. The *Nautilus*
C. The *Beagle*
D. The *Galapagos*

$32,000

In 1917, America purchased what are now known as the U.S. Virgin Islands from which country?

A. Spain
B. Denmark
C. Portugal
D. England

$64,000

Who of the following was not a five-star general?

A. Douglas MacArthur
B. George S. Patton
C. Dwight D. Eisenhower
D. Omar Nelson Bradley

$16,000

A or C

$125,000

What is the name of the queen and wife of Pharaoh Akhenaton?

A. Nefertiti
B. Cleopatra
C. Nefertari
D. Alexandria

$32,000

B or C

$250,000

In the book *The Legend of Sleepy Hollow,* what is the name of Ichabod Crane's horse?

A. Old England
B. Buttermilk
C. Shadowfax
D. Gunpowder

50:50
B or D

$500,000

What is the only planet in our solar system that rotates clockwise?

A. Venus
B. Earth
C. Jupiter
D. Saturn

$125,000

50:50
A or C

$1,000,000

Which composer wrote
The Hebrides Overture, also
known as *Fingal's Cave*?

A. Felix Mendelssohn
B. Benjamin Britten
C. Edvard Grieg
D. Ludwig van Beethoven

$250,000

B or D

$500,000

A or D

$100

On what part of a letter or
postcard is it appropriate to affix
a stamp?

A. Lower right-hand corner
B. Upper right-hand corner
C. Lower left-hand corner
D. Upper left-hand corner

$200

Lynx, Russian Blue and Abyssinian
are all breeds of which animal?

$1,000,000

50:50

A or D

A. Dogs
B. Cats
C. Horses
D. Rabbits

$300

Who of the following helped save the Chrysler Corporation and wrote an autobiography that sold several million copies?

A. Henry Ford, Jr.
B. John DeLorean
C. Lee Iacocca
D. Joe Isuzu

$100

(50:50)

B or D

$500

Which of the following is not a popular boy band?

A. N' Sync
B. 98 Degrees
C. Go Dogs Go
D. Backstreet Boys

$200

(50:50)

B or D

$1,000

Television's Judge Judy was originally a Family Court judge in which U.S. city?

A. New York
B. Boston
C. Philadelphia
D. Chicago

B or C

$2,000

Which of the following is a perfect score on the College Board's Scholastic Assessment Test?

A. 1000
B. 1200
C. 1600
D. 2000

B or C

$4,000

Which of the following is another word for dandruff?

A. Scurf
B. Scruff
C. Sprue
D. Ich

A or C

$8,000

Which month is named for the Roman god of war?

A. January
B. March
C. May
D. October

B or C

$16,000

What were movie theater audiences encouraged to use while watching the John Waters's movie *Polyester*?

A. Headphones
B. 3-D glasses
C. Scratch-and-sniff cards
D. Tomatoes

$4,000

A or C

$32,000

Why was the originally gray-colored Executive Mansion—later called the White House—painted white after the War of 1812?

A. To cover up burn marks
B. To suit Abigail Adams
C. To celebrate Easter
D. To camouflage in winter

$8,000

B or C

$64,000

Which of the following is not a trademarked name?

A. Velcro
B. Band-Aid
C. Frisbee
D. Mayonnaise

$16,000

50:50

B or C

$125,000

Who was the first American to go outside an orbiting spacecraft, attached only by a tether?

A. John Glenn
B. Alan Shepard
C. Ed White
D. Gus Grissom

$32,000

50:50

A or B

$250,000

Which of the following was the only Gilbert and Sullivan operetta to open in New York City before London?

A. *Pirates of Penzance*
B. *The H.M.S. Pinafore*
C. *The Sorcerer*
D. *Princess Ida*

B or D

$500,000

What was the given family name of President Bill Clinton before he formally changed it at age fifteen?

A. Blythe
B. Oxford
C. LaPlante
D. Wood

50:50

B or C

$1,000,000

The Rock of Gibraltar is composed primarily of what type of stone?

A. Limestone
B. Granite
C. Basalt
D. Schist

$250,000

50:50

A or B

$500,000

50:50

A or C

GAME 5

$100

What candies take their name from the company's cofounders, Forrest Mars and Bruce Murrie?

A. M&M's
B. Snickers
C. 3 Musketeers
D. Reese's Pieces

$200

If it's 11 P.M. in Seattle, Washington, what time is it in Miami, Florida?

A. 1 A.M.
B. 8 P.M.
C. 3 A.M.
D. 2 A.M.

$1,000,000

50:50

A or B

$300

Which of the following toy stores is featured in the movie *Big*?

A. Kay-Bee
B. Toys 'R' Us
C. F.A.O. Schwarz
D. Child World

$100

50:50

A or D

$500

What animal lives in a "warren"?

A. Rabbit
B. Opossum
C. Snake
D. Beaver

$200

50:50

A or D

$1,000

In the television series *Home Improvement,* what is the name of the home-repair show hosted by main character Tim Taylor?

A. Tools & Power
B. The Power Hour
C. Tool Time
D. Hammer Time

$2,000

"The Defense of Fort McHenry" was the original title of what song?

A. "Battle Hymn of the Republic"
B. "Over There"
C. "Onward, Christian Soldiers"
D. "The Star-Spangled Banner"

$4,000

How is your posture described if you're standing with hands on hips and elbows bent outward?

A. Cross-purposed
B. Sejeant
C. Courant
D. Akimbo

$1,000

50:50
A or C

$8,000

The play *Inherit the Wind* is a fictionalized account of which famous 1920s trial?

$2,000

50:50
A or D

A. Scottsboro boys
B. Scopes "monkey"
C. Sacco and Vanzetti
D. Leopold and Loeb

$16,000

Which of the following is not a beach at Normandy?

A. Juno
B. Utah
C. Sword
D. Saber

$4,000

B or D

$32,000

In the fourth century B.C., Egypt's King Ptolemy I oversaw the creation of what object in Alexandria?

A. Sphinx
B. Temple
C. Library
D. Wall

$8,000

A or B

$64,000

What U.S. state capital's primary access is by air or water?

A. Olympia
B. Juneau
C. Baton Rouge
D. Honolulu

$16,000
50:50
C or D

$125,000

In 1961, what hung upside-down at New York's Museum of Modern Art for more than a month before someone noticed the mistake?

A. A 25,000 pound mobile
B. A Henri Matisse painting
C. A Mondrian painting
D. The "Mona Lisa"

$32,000
50:50
A or C

$250,000

Where can the "Maxwell Gap" be found?

A. Mars
B. The asteroid belt
C. Halley's comet
D. Saturn's rings

$64,000

50:50

B or D

$500,000

What country's national flag is not in the shape of a rectangle?

A. Nepal
B. Qatar
C. Guyana
D. Liechtenstein

$125,000

50:50

B or D

$1,000,000

In Mozart's opera *Don Giovanni*, how many lovers does Leporello claim Don Giovanni has had in Spain?

A. 156
B. 849
C. 1,003
D. 3,727

$250,000

B or D

$500,000

A or B

$100

As of November 1999, what is the name of the current CEO of Microsoft?

A. Bill Gates
B. Bob Bates
C. Bob Gates
D. Steve Jobs

$200

Counting upwards one number at a time starting with zero, what is the fifth number that begins with the letter "T"?

$1,000,000

(50:50)

B or C

A. Twelve
B. Thirteen
C. Twenty
D. Twenty-one

$300

Which of the following artists was primarily known as a sculptor?

A. Auguste Rodin
B. Auguste Renoir
C. Claude Monet
D. Georgia O'Keeffe

$100

50:50

A or D

$500

In 1999, Grammy-winner Brandy starred in which of the following television sitcoms?

$200

50:50

B or C

A. *Sister, Sister*
B. *Cosby*
C. *Living Single*
D. *Moesha*

$1,000

What positions make up the battery in baseball?

A. Pitcher and catcher
B. Shortstop and second base
C. First and third base
D. Left field, center field, and right field

$300

50:50
A or B

$2,000

What fruit introduced to Europe in the mid-1500s was known as the "gold apple" in Italy and the "love apple" in France?

$500

A. Orange
B. Apple
C. Banana
D. Tomato

50:50
A or D

$4,000

The term "vis-à-vis" comes from the French words for what?

A. Head-to-head
B. This-to-this
C. Face-to-face
D. Thing-to-thing

$1,000

50:50

A or B

$8,000

In both 1936 and 1937, what was the best-selling novel in the United States?

$2,000

50:50

A or D

A. *The Good Earth*
B. *Ship of Fools*
C. *The Robe*
D. *Gone with the Wind*

$16,000

What type of building structure is a mansard?

A. Stairwell
B. Roof
C. Basement
D. Hallway

$4,000

B or C

$32,000

Who is the only person to win a Nobel prize in both physics and chemistry?

A. Marie Curie
B. Linus Pauling
C. Albert Einstein
D. Francis Crick

$8,000

A or D

$64,000

Which two U.S. presidents both died on July 4, 1826?

A. James Madison, James Monroe

B. Thomas Jefferson, John Adams

C. George Washington, Andrew Jackson

D. James Monroe, John Quincy Adams

$16,000

50:50

A or B

$125,000

Which of the following philosophers predates the rest?

$32,000

50:50

A or C

A. Aristotle

B. Epicurus

C. Plato

D. Socrates

$250,000

According to scientific theory, the planets of our solar system were formed from what early cosmic bodies?

A. Planetesimals
B. Orbules
C. Spheriloids
D. Seminorbs

B or D

$500,000

What song won the first and only Grammy Award for Best Disco Recording?

A. "Hot Stuff"
B. "Stayin' Alive"
C. "I Will Survive"
D. "The Hustle"

A or D

$1,000,000

Located in southern England, what massive work of art is carved into the side of a hill?

A. Great Man of Oxfordshire

B. Dancers at Glenfiddich

C. The White Horse of Uffington

D. The Dog of East Llanwynn

$250,000

50:50

A or B

$500,000

50:50

B or C

· GAME 7 ·

$100

On which holiday weekend does comedian Jerry Lewis usually host his annual telethon?

A. Memorial Day
B. Labor Day
C. Easter
D. Earth Day

$200

What does the abbreviation "P.S." at the bottom of a letter stand for?

A. Plus such
B. Post scriptum
C. Private section
D. Please see

$1.000.000

50:50
A or C

$300

Considered a dessert delicacy in Elizabethan times, a pippin is what type of food?

A. Apple
B. Nectarine
C. Pear
D. Pastry

$100

50:50

A or B

$500

Which of the following authors based the characters in *Winnie the Pooh* on his son and the boy's stuffed animals?

A. J. K. Rowling
B. A. A. Milne
C. E. B. White
D. J. M. Barrie

$200

50:50

B or D

$1,000

Which prime-time television soap opera centered on the lives of the Carrington family?

A. *Falcon Crest*

B. *Dynasty*

C. *Dallas*

D. *Knots Landing*

$300

A or B

$2,000

In a 1982 song by the band Tommy Tutone, what was "Jenny's" number?

A. 853-5937

B. 867-5309

C. 634-5789

D. 1-800-99-JENNY

$500

A or B

$4,000

What "line" runs through Greenwich, England, and is responsible for standardizing world time?

A. Equator
B. Prime meridian
C. 38th parallel
D. International Date Line

$1,000

A or B

$8,000

Which historic disaster led a reporter to exclaim, "Oh the humanity"?

$2,000

B or C

A. Sinking of the *Titanic*
B. *Hindenburg* explosion
C. Chicago fire of 1871
D. San Francisco earthquake of 1906

$16,000

Which cartoonist created the donkey and elephant as symbols of the United States' two major political parties?

A. Thomas Nast
B. Pat Oliphant
C. Tom Toles
D. Al Hirschfeld

$4,000

50:50
B or C

$32,000

Where is Manet's "Portrait of Mademoiselle Suzette Lemaire, in Profile" displayed?

A. Le Louvre
B. Metropolitan Mueseum of Art
C. The Bellagio Gallery of Fine Art
D. Trump Tower

$8,000

50:50
A or B

$64,000

In what country was South American freedom fighter Simon Bolivar born?

A. Peru
B. Colombia
C. Bolivia
D. Venezuela

$16,000

50:50

A or B

$125,000

What was the first full-length major studio feature that was filmed entirely in 3-D?

$32,000

50:50

A or C

A. *Bwana Devil*
B. *House of Wax*
C. *The Raven*
D. *Custer's Last Stand*

$250,000

What is the name of the non-existent chemical once believed to be emitted when objects burned?

A. Phlogiston
B. Epoxyhydride
C. Plasma
D. Ignision

C or D

$500,000

Who said the assassination of JFK was a case of "the chickens coming home to roost"?

A. Fidel Castro
B. Malcolm X
C. J. Edgar Hoover
D. Bobby Seale

A or B

$1,000,000

Which of the following words is not one of the approximately 1,700 first put into print by Shakespeare?

A. Assassination
B. Listen
C. Auspicious
D. Bumper

$250,000

A or C

$500,000

B or C

GAME 8

$100

What substance causes Superman to lose his powers?

A. Lead
B. Admantium
C. Kryptonite
D. Caffeine

$200

What is the thirteenth consonant in the modern English alphabet?

A. N
B. Q
C. O
D. P

B or C

$300

In which baseball park does the fabled "Green Monster" tower over left field?

A. Comiskey
B. Fenway
C. Wrigley
D. Hershey

$100

50:50

B or C

$500

Naturalist John James Audubon is notable for his paintings and illustrations of which of the following?

$200

50:50

A or B

A. Horses
B. Birds
C. Presidents
D. Street urchins

$1,000

For over seventy-five years, which of these products has used as its motto "When It Rains, It Pours"?

A. Morton Salt
B. Campbell's Soup
C. Bumble Bee tuna
D. Sun-Maid raisins

$2,000

WWF wrestler "Stone Cold" Steve Austin is known for having what biblical reference printed on his T-shirts?

A. 2:10
B. 3:16
C. 5:14
D. 9:11

$4,000

The opera *Aida*, set in the era of the pharaohs, was staged in October 1999 at the foot of what nation's Great Pyramids?

A. Saudi Arabia
B. Libya
C. Egypt
D. Morocco

A or B

$8,000

The headwaters of the Mississippi River are in which state?

A. Louisiana
B. Michigan
C. Minnesota
D. Missouri

B or C

$16,000

Who wrote "East is East, and West is West, and never the twain shall meet"?

A. Emily Dickinson
B. Mark Twain
C. Ralph Waldo Emerson
D. Rudyard Kipling

C or D

$32,000

The Empire State Building is an example of what style of architecture?

A. Gothic
B. Classical
C. Art Deco
D. Postmodern

B or C

$64,000

What crime syndicate godfather allegedly boasted, "We're bigger than U.S. Steel"?

A. Bugsy Siegel
B. Meyer Lansky
C. Lucky Luciano
D. Arnold Rothstein

C or D

$125,000

What American artist created a famous series of paintings featuring the U.S. flag?

A. Roy Lichtenstein
B. Andy Warhol
C. Jackson Pollock
D. Jasper Johns

$250,000

Who was the only person to have ever held the rank "General of the Armies" while he was alive?

A. John J. Pershing
B. George Washington
C. Douglas MacArthur
D. Dwight Eisenhower

$64,000

50:50
B or C

$500,000

According to legend, what ancient Greek playwright died when an eagle dropped a turtle on his head?

A. Aeschylus
B. Euripides
C. Sophocles
D. Hesiod

$125,000

50:50
B or D

$1,000,000

What physicist discovered the existence of atomic nuclei?

A. Niels Bohr

B. Robert Oppenheimer

C. Max Planck

D. Ernest Rutherford

$250,000

A or B

$500,000

A or C

GAME 9

$100

According to superstition, if spilled, which of the following items should you throw over your left shoulder to avoid bad luck?

A. Sweet'N Low
B. Sugar
C. Salt
D. Pepper

$200

What are the professions of Cliff and Clair Huxtable in the TV series *The Cosby Show*?

 $1.000.000
 50:50
C or D

A. Teacher and lawyer
B. Doctor and cartoonist
C. Doctor and lawyer
D. Lawyer and jazz musician

$300

What hour, mentioned in the Bible, has come to mean the last possible moment that something can be done?

    A. 10th
    B. 11th
    C. 12th
    D. 13th

B or C

$500

In the title of a 1950s Chuck Berry song, what classical composer is asked to "roll over"?

    A. Mozart
    B. Schubert
    C. Beethoven
    D. Bach

A or C

$1,000

What is the specific term for a horse's female parent?

A. Foal
B. Mare
C. Filly
D. Dam

$2,000

What natural resource is known as "black gold"?

A. Petroleum
B. Diamonds
C. Coal
D. Iron

$300

B or D

$500

A or C

$4,000

What singer's name is an anagram of "Presbyterians"?

A. Britney Spears
B. Robert Preston
C. Peabo Bryson
D. Bernadette Peters

$8,000

Which of the following assassins was not attempting to kill a United States president?

A. Lee Harvey Oswald
B. Sirhan Sirhan
C. John Wilkes Booth
D. Leon Czolgosz

$16,000

Alaska's Mt. McKinley is part of which national park?

A. Glacier Bay
B. Gates of the Arctic
C. Kenai Fjords
D. Denali

$4,000

A or C

$32,000

What is the proper thing to do with a calash?

A. Eat it
B. Invest it
C. Ride in it
D. Smoke it

$8,000

B or D

$64,000

Which of the following was the first national nonsectarian organization for girls in America?

A. Camp Fire Girls
B. Girls Club of America
C. Girls State
D. Girl Scouts

$16,000
50:50
A or D

$125,000

What fictional spy is named after a Philadelphia ornithologist who wrote *Birds of the West Indies*?

A. James Bond
B. George Smiley
C. Napoleon Solo
D. Alexander Scott

$32,000
50:50
C or D

$250,000

Which of the following directions is also known as "withershins" or "widdershins"?

A. Clockwise
B. Counterclockwise
C. Due north
D. Zigzag

$64,000

50:50

A or C

$500,000

On the Great Seal of the United States, what is the eagle holding in its beak?

A. Olive branch
B. Ribbon
C. Arrows of war
D. Flag

$125,000

50:50

A or D

$1,000,000

The Kurt Weill/Maxwell Anderson musical *Lost in the Stars* was based on what 1948 best-selling novel?

A. *Invisible Man*

B. *Cry, the Beloved Country*

C. *Native Son*

D. *Black Like Me*

$250,000

B or D

$500,000

A or B

GAME 10

$100

According to the slogan that begins "Like a good neighbor...," which insurance company "is there"?

A. Prudential
B. MetLife
C. State Farm
D. Allstate

$200

Which of the following is found inside an "Eskimo Pie"?

A. Whale blubber
B. Ice cream
C. Caribou meat
D. An Eskimo

$1,000,000

50:50

B or C

$300

Which of the following words is a pronoun?

A. Which
B. Of
C. The
D. Following

$100
50:50
C or D

$500

Eloise, the title character in Kay Thompson's children's book series, lives in which New York City hotel?

$200
50:50
A or B

A. The Plaza
B. The St. Regis
C. The Pierre
D. The Waldorf-Astoria

$1,000

Which of the following actors never starred as a "Blues Brother" on film?

A. John Belushi
B. John Goodman
C. Bill Murray
D. Dan Aykroyd

$300

50:50
A or B

$2,000

What French designer became known in the 1920s for combining masculine tailoring with women's clothing?

A. Yves Saint-Laurent
B. Coco Chanel
C. Christian Dior
D. Claire McCardell

$500

50:50
A or D

$4,000

Which of the following countries was not an ally of the United States during World War II?

A. Iran
B. Turkey
C. Liberia
D. Finland

$1,000

50:50

B or C

$8,000

What was the nickname for the original Tacoma Narrows bridge?

A. Galloping Gertie
B. Shaking Sally
C. Trembling Terry
D. Wavy Gravy

$2,000

50:50

A or B

$16,000

What All-American football player
and member of Phi Beta Kappa
immortalized the Broadway song
"Ol' Man River"?

A. Ving Rhames
B. James Earl Jones
C. Gregory Hines
D. Paul Robeson

$4,000

50:50
A or D

$32,000

An artist who uses tesserae would
be most likely to create what?

A. An oil painting
B. Pottery
C. A mosaic
D. A screenplay

$8,000

50:50
A or B

$64,000

What company, founded over two hundred years ago, dropped door-to-door sales in 1996?

A. Amway
B. Fuller Brush
C. Avon
D. Encyclopedia Britannica

$16,000

50:50
B or D

$125,000

In the U.S., if a patriotic orator is practicing "spread-eagleism," what would he be labeled?

$32,000

50:50
B or C

A. Abolitionist
B. Jingoist
C. Fascist
D. Expansionist

$250,000

Who was the founder of Stoicism?

A. Zeno of Citium
B. Epictetus
C. Marcus Aurelius
D. Diogenes

$64,000

50:50

B or D

$500,000

What political movement did
L. Frank Baum satirize in his 1904
book, *The Marvelous Land of Oz*?

A. Woman suffrage
B. Temperance
C. Labor
D. Urban reform

$125,000

50:50

B or D

$1,000,000

Which of the following lakes borders the most countries?

A. Lake Nyasa
B. Lake Baikal
C. Lake Tanganyika
D. Lake Victoria

$250,000

A or C

$500,000

50:50

A or D

· GAME 11 ·

$100

What color is an emerald?

A. Green
B. Red
C. Clear
D. Purple

$200

Which of the following is not a character on *Sesame Street*?

A. Cookie Monster
B. Grimace
C. Bert
D. Big Bird

$1,000,000

50:50
C or D

$300

The White House Easter-egg roll can only occur during what two months?

A. February and March
B. March and April
C. April and May
D. May and June

$100

A or C

$500

Who did the Continental Congress appoint as the first postmaster general in 1775?

$200

B or C

A. Alexander Hamilton
B. John Adams
C. Benjamin Franklin
D. Thomas Jefferson

$1,000

How many striped balls are used in a game of eightball?

A. 4
B. 7
C. 8
D. 15

$300

B or C

$2,000

By definition, the need to set fires means you are suffering from what compulsion?

A. Pyromania
B. Dipsomania
C. Kleptomania
D. Nymphomania

$500

A or C

$4,000

Which one of the following classical musicians is not a renowned violinist?

A. Itzhak Perlman
B. Isaac Stern
C. Yehudi Menuhin
D. Yo-Yo Ma

$1,000

B or C

$8,000

Where would you most likely find the animal known as a kestrel?

A. Air

$2,000

A or B

B. Underground
C. Outer space
D. Underwater

$16,000

About one-third of all silver is consumed by which of the following industries?

A. Pharmaceutical
B. Photographic
C. Computer manufacturing
D. Car manufacturing

$4,000

C or D

$32,000

Enjoyed by the widows of former presidents, what are "franking" privileges?

A. Free postage
B. Free parking
C. Free bodyguards
D. Free rent

$8,000

A or C

$64,000

Which of the following is the correct spelling of a Stephen King bestseller?

A. *Pet Semetery*

B. *Pet Semetary*

C. *Pet Sematary*

D. *Pet Sematery*

B or C

$125,000

Who choreographed ballets that were usually plotless and often performed in practice clothes?

A. Martha Graham

B. Marius Petipa

C. Sergei Diaghilev

D. George Balanchine

A or C

$250,000

When standing watch at sea, when is the "first dogwatch"?

A. 8 P.M. to midnight
B. Midnight to 4 A.M.
C. 4 A.M. to 8 A.M.
D. 4 P.M. to 6 P.M.

B or C

$500,000

What author was also a clergyman and served as dean of St. Patrick's Cathedral in Dublin?

A. Jonathan Swift
B. William Congreve
C. John Dryden
D. Richard Sheridan

A or D

$1,000,000

To what political party did Andrew Johnson belong when he was elected Abraham Lincoln's vice president?

A. Democrat
B. Democrat-Republican
C. Whig
D. National Union Party

$250,000

50:50
B or D

$500,000

50:50
A or C

· GAME 12 ·

$100

What does ATM stand for?

A. Automated Teller Machine
B. Autonomic Teller Machine
C. Automatically to Money
D. All the Moolah

$200

According to the American folk song, which of the following can be found "on top of Old Smoky"?

A. Snow
B. Flowers
C. Bears
D. Trees

$1,000,000

B or D

$300

In a legislative body, what is it called when someone blocks passage of a bill with tactics such as long speeches?

A. Filibuster
B. Sequester
C. Legibuster
D. Capitol kill

$100

50:50

A or B

$500

Who was the villainous pirate in the book *Treasure Island*?

A. Bluebeard
B. Blackbeard
C. Long John Silver
D. Captain Hook

$200
50:50

A or C

$1,000

In 1983, David Copperfield performed the "illusion of the century" when he made what disappear?

A. The Washington Monument
B. The Empire State Building
C. Gorbachev's birthmark
D. The Statue of Liberty

A or B

$2,000

In a standard deck of playing cards, how many face cards have figures with only one eye showing?

A. 1
B. 2
C. 3
D. 4

B or C

$4,000

As of 1999, which of the following television shows had not been spun off into a feature film?

A. *Leave It to Beaver*
B. *Sergeant Bilko*
C. *Wonder Woman*
D. *Lost in Space*

$1,000

50:50

A or D

$8,000

In 1993, who presented an original poem at the inauguration of President Clinton?

A. Allen Ginsberg
B. Robert Pinsky
C. Maya Angelou
D. Jewel

$2,000

50:50

B or C

$16,000

The coffee chain Starbucks got its name from a character in what novel?

A. *Moby-Dick*

B. *Dracula*

C. *Treasure Island*

D. *A Tale of Two Cities*

$4,000

50:50
A or C

$32,000

Which of the following women coined the phrase "birth control"?

A. Dorothea Dix

B. Dorothy Day

C. Margaret Sanger

D. Jane Addams

$8,000

50:50
A or C

$64,000

What was the name of the first manned American space capsule?

A. *Freedom 7*
B. *Apollo 13*
C. *Friendship 10*
D. *Gemini 3*

$16,000

A or C

$125,000

What scientist is known for saying, "God does not play dice with the universe"?

$32,000

C or D

A. Carl Sagan
B. Albert Einstein
C. Isaac Newton
D. Copernicus

$250,000

The eerie sounds of what musical instrument can be heard in Alfred Hitchcock's *Spellbound* and the Beach Boys' "Good Vibrations"?

A. Mellotron
B. Theremin
C. Moog synthesizer
D. Clavivox

 50:50

A or C

$500,000

What is the common term for metempsychosis?

A. Nervous breakdown
B. Reincarnation
C. Love
D. Exorcism

 50:50

B or C

$1,000,000

Whose design masterpiece are the gardens at Versailles?

A. André Le Nôtre
B. Claude Perrault
C. Pierre L'Enfant
D. Louis Le Vau

$250,000

50:50

B or C

$500,000

50:50

B or D

GAME 13

$100

Each Halloween, whose arrival
does the comic-strip character
Linus eagerly await?

A. The Great Gourd
B. The Mighty Pumpkin
C. Super Pumpkin
D. The Great Pumpkin

$200

"Gridiron" is a name for the
playing field of what sport?

A. Baseball
B. Football
C. Soccer
D. Lacrosse

$1,000,000

50:50
A or D

$300

Who is the mascot of Planters Nuts?

A. Ellie Elephant
B. Chunky P. Nut
C. Nutley
D. Mr. Peanut

$100

50:50

B or D

$500

What did scientists use to clone dinosaurs in the movie *Jurassic Park*?

$200

50:50

A or B

A. Witch's brew
B. Time machine
C. Prehistoric DNA
D. Computer graphics

$1,000

In which part of the human body would you find the iris?

A. Ears
B. Eyes
C. Hair
D. Nose

$2,000

Which of the following words is spelled correctly?

A. Rediculous
B. Mispelled
C. Embarass
D. Judgment

$300

B or D

$500

C or D

$4,000

Which of the following airports is named after a pilot who shot down airplanes in World War II?

A. O'Hare
B. La Guardia
C. Logan
D. Dulles

A or B

$8,000

By definition, what is a "cruciverbalist" concerned with?

A. Sermons
B. Vegetables
C. Biographies
D. Crosswords

B or D

$16,000

What was the first company traded on the New York Stock Exchange?

A. J. P. Morgan
B. Bank of New York
C. General Motors
D. General Electric

$4,000

A or C

$32,000

What American journalist did Warren Beatty portray in the film *Reds*?

A. Max Eastman
B. Eugene O'Neill
C. John Reed
D. William Inge

$8,000

A or D

$64,000

The geographic center of the United States, including Alaska and Hawaii, is located in which state?

A. South Dakota
B. Nebraska
C. Idaho
D. Kansas

$16,000

B or D

$125,000

The names of the main characters in the Edward Albee play *Who's Afraid of Virginia Woolf?* are the same as which presidential couple?

$32,000

A or C

A. The Nixons
B. The Washingtons
C. The Trumans
D. The Lincolns

$250,000

The Academy of Sciences of which country is credited with creating the metric system?

A. Italy

B. France

C. Great Britain

D. Germany

$500,000

Wahhabi is a sub-sect of what religion?

A. Islam

B. Jainism

C. Hinduism

D. Rastafarianism

$1,000,000

Having lost the Battle of Point Pleasant in 1774, what Cayuga chief "lamented" over the white man's treachery?

A. Tachnechdorus

B. Menawa

C. Matonabbee

D. Canassatego

$250,000

B or D

$500,000

A or C

• GAME 14 •

$100

What toy was discovered in 1945 after a spring used on battleships fell and tumbled end over end across the floor?

A. Pogo stick
B. Rubik's Cube
C. Slinky
D. Silly Putty

$200

What kind of frog-hating animals can be found in the ad campaign for Budweiser beer?

A. Flies
B. Lizards
C. Snakes
D. Elk

$1,000,000

50:50

A or D

$300

What fictional Alaska town was the setting for the popular TV series *Northern Exposure*?

A. Rome
B. Anchorage
C. Cicely
D. Mystery

$100

50:50
A or C

$500

Who was the first American woman to travel into outer space?

A. Sally Ride
B. Eileen Collins
C. Mary Cleave
D. Farrah Fawcett

$200

50:50
A or B

$1,000

What is the name of the magical world created by author C. S. Lewis to which characters travel through the back of a wardrobe?

A. Xanadu
B. The Island of Dr. Moreau
C. Loompaland
D. Narnia

$300

50:50
C or D

$2,000

In the movie *Saturday Night Fever*, where does main character Tony Manero live?

A. Queens
B. Brooklyn
C. Staten Island
D. Bronx

$500

50:50
A or C

$4,000

What painting style deceives the eye with a convincing illusion of 3-D reality?

A. Watercolor
B. Grisaille
C. Pointillism
D. Trompe l'oeil

$1,000
50:50
A or D

$8,000

What organization has the symbol and reverse colors of the Swiss flag?

$2,000
50:50
A or B

A. NATO
B. United Nations
C. OPEC
D. American Red Cross

$16,000

The Jurassic period was part of which geologic era?

A. Paleozoic
B. Mesozoic
C. Cenozoic
D. Disco

$4,000

B or D

$32,000

In what sport is Janet Evans an Olympic gold medalist?

A. Speed skating
B. Diving
C. Swimming
D. Track and field

$8,000

A or D

$64,000

Which of the following United States vice presidents served as "acting president" for about eight hours?

A. Walter Mondale
B. Lyndon Johnson
C. George Bush
D. Nelson Rockefeller

$16.000

50:50

B or C

$125,000

Labanotation is a system that uses symbols on a staff to record what?

A. Dance movements
B. Lip reading
C. Oral history
D. Medical condition

$32.000

50:50

A or C

$250,000

Which of the following people won a Republican seat in the Connecticut state legislature in 1865?

A. Lewis Carroll
B. P. T. Barnum
C. William Tecumseh Sherman
D. Harriet Tubman

$500,000

The Louvre Museum was originally constructed as a fortress under which French king?

A. Louis XIII
B. Phillipe I
C. Phillipe II Augustus
D. Louis XV

$1,000,000

How long does it take the light from the sun to reach the Earth?

A. 42 seconds
B. 3 minutes
C. 8 minutes
D. 1 hour

$250,000

50:50

A or B

$500,000

50:50

A or C

· GAME 15 ·

$100

According to the seventeenth-century proverb, if March comes in like a lion, what does it go out like?

A. Fawn
B. Lamb
C. Breeze
D. Baby

$200

What does England call its police officers?

A. Bobbies
B. Tommies
C. Jimmies
D. Johnnies

$1,000,000

50:50
A or C

$300

What is the traditional cocktail of the Kentucky Derby?

A. South Side
B. Boilermaker
C. Whiskey Sour
D. Mint Julep

$100

50:50
A or B

$500

Where does the literary character "The Hobbit" live?

A. South Philly
B. The Shire
C. South Wales
D. The Valley of the Ents

$200
50:50
A or B

$1,000

Who was the first woman to anchor a major television network's national nightly news broadcast?

A. Diane Sawyer
B. Barbara Walters
C. Connie Chung
D. Deborah Norville

A or D

$2,000

Which of the following will speed up the rate of a chemical reaction?

A. Isomer
B. Catalyst
C. Polymer
D. Isotope

B or D

$4,000

If you combine the abbreviations for centrigrade, before noon, and earned run average, what word do you get?

A. Center
B. Cinema
C. Camera
D. Chimera

B or C

$8,000

Which of these initially developed what is now known as the Internet?

A. Microsoft
B. Department of Defense
C. NASA
D. George Lucas

B or C

$16,000

Which child star penned the autobiography *Little Girl Lost* at the age of 14?

A. Judy Garland
B. Drew Barrymore
C. Gloria Vanderbilt
D. Shirley Temple

$4,000

50:50

C or D

$32,000

Catgut, once commonly used to string tennis rackets, comes from the intestines of what animal?

A. Cat
B. Sheep
C. Dog
D. Cow

$8,000

50:50

B or C

$64,000

Which of the following is accurate regarding the status of Puerto Rican nationals?

A. Pay U.S. taxes
B. Can be drafted by U.S. Army
C. Can vote in U.S.
D. Are not U.S. citizens

$16,000

50:50

B or C

$125,000

What was Francis Scott Key's profession?

A. Lawyer
B. Soldier
C. Shipbuilder
D. Dockworker

$32,000

50:50

B or D

$250,000

What unit of measure equals 1/100th of a second?

A. Snap
B. Jiffy
C. Sec
D. Shake of a lamb's tail

$64,000

A or B

$500,000

According to legend, what discovery led Archimedes to run naked through town shouting "Eureka"?

$125,000

A or C

A. Plasma theory
B. Photoelectric effect
C. Principle of buoyancy
D. Law of wave motion

$1,000,000

Whose face adorned the first U.S. coin to bear the likeness of a foreign monarch?

A. Charles II
B. Queen Victoria
C. Queen Isabella
D. King Ferdinand

$250,000

A or B

$500,000

C or D

GAME 16

$100

What location in Colorado is known as the "Mile High City"?

A. Boulder
B. Denver
C. Aspen
D. Golden

$200

As of 1999, which of the following was not a search engine on the Internet?

A. Yahoo
B. Amazon
C. Alta Vista
D. Lycos

50:50
C or D

$1,000,000

$300

Which evening newscaster consistently ended his broadcasts with the phrase, "And that's the way it is"?

A. Edward R. Murrow
B. Walter Cronkite
C. Dennis Miller
D. Dan Rather

A or B

$500

What is the nickname of Bad Boy Entertainment's president Sean Combs?

A. Kid Rock
B. Dr. Nice
C. Puffy
D. Shasta McNasty

$1,000

What does it mean to dine "alfresco"?

A. Eat outside
B. Eat light
C. Eat Italian
D. Eat raw food

$300

50:50
A or B

$2,000

What is the total of the number of days in a week plus a baker's dozen plus the number of stars on a current U.S. flag?

A. 33
B. 68
C. 69
D. 70

$500

50:50
A or C

$4,000

Which country was the first to send a woman into space?

A. Soviet Union
B. China
C. United States
D. Germany

$1,000

50:50

A or B

$8,000

By which method did artist Jackson Pollock like to apply paint to a canvas?

$2,000

50:50

C or D

A. Spin
B. Drip
C. Point
D. Crane

$16,000

The annual advertising award the Clio is named after the Greek Muse of what discipline?

A. History
B. Sacred poetry
C. Epic poetry
D. Comedy

$32,000

In what U.S. state will you find the colorful sandstone formations called the Painted Desert?

A. Arizona
B. Texas
C. New Mexico
D. California

$64,000

What was Pulitzer Prize–winning author Frank McCourt's job for most of his forty-five years in New York?

A. Social worker
B. Teacher
C. Columnist
D. Bartender

50:50

A or C

$125,000

About how much water can a ten-gallon hat hold?

A. One pint
B. Three quarts
C. Two gallons
D. Ten gallons

50:50

A or C

$250,000

In Mexico, the Cinco de Mayo holiday celebrates an 1862 battle in which Mexican troops defeated soldiers from what country?

A. Spain
B. France
C. United States
D. England

B or C

$500,000

In which of the following nations do the natives have surnames, but not family names?

A. El Salvador
B. Rwanda
C. Iceland
D. Pakistan

B or C

$1,000,000

Whose revolutionary theorem proved that no mathematical system is immune to paradoxes?

A. Kurt Gödel
B. Werner Heisenberg
C. Erwin Schrodinger
D. Max Born

$250,000

B or C

$500,000

B or C

· GAME 17 ·

$100

A "bumper crop" is what kind
of harvest?

A. Spring
B. Abundant
C. Ruined
D. Early

$200

Who sang lead for the 1960s girl
group The Supremes?

A. Diana Ross
B. Gladys Knight
C. Aretha Franklin
D. Dionne Warwick

$1,000,000

(50:50)

A or D

$300

How many black dots are there in total on a standard die?

A. 15
B. 18
C. 21
D. 24

$500

What relation to me is my mother's father's only daughter?

A. Mother
B. Cousin
C. Sister
D. Aunt

$1,000

Before getting their own prime-time show, characters Laverne and Shirley appeared briefly on which TV series?

A. *Mork and Mindy*
B. *All in the Family*
C. *Happy Days*
D. *The Bob Newhart Show*

$300

(50:50) B or C

$2,000

What word is derived from the Latin meaning "where three roads meet"?

A. Fork
B. Trivia
C. Slingshot
D. Hexagon

$500

(50:50) A or D

$4,000

In the nineteenth century,
what did a phrenologist study in
order to find out more about a
person's character?

A. Hands
B. Skull
C. Feet
D. Stomach

$1,000

A or C

$8,000

Picasso at the Lapin Agile was the
first published original play
written by which of the following
comedians?

$2,000

A or B

A. Bill Murray
B. Nathan Lane
C. Martin Short
D. Steve Martin

$16,000

Which of the following foods is not a major source of vitamin C?

A. Carrot
B. Cabbage
C. Tomato
D. Strawberries

$4,000

50:50
B or D

$32,000

Which of these buildings is most likely to have a qibla wall?

A. Mosque
B. Cathedral
C. Greek temple
D. Synagogue

$8,000

50:50
B or D

$64,000

Who held the first presidential news conference from which the press was allowed to make direct quotations?

A. Abraham Lincoln
B. Theodore Roosevelt
C. Dwight D. Eisenhower
D. John F. Kennedy

A or D

$125,000

Before donating her life savings of $150,000 to the University of Southern Mississippi, what was Oseola McCarthy's job?

A. Teacher
B. Laundress
C. Waitress
D. Crossing guard

A or C

$250,000

What did John Wilkes Booth shout to the crowd in Ford's Theater after shooting Lincoln?

A. "Veni vidi vici!"
B. "Semper fidelis!"
C. "Sic semper tyrannis!"
D. "Cogito ergo sum!"

$64,000

50:50

B or C

$500,000

Which of the following is found in RNA and not in DNA?

A. Adenine
B. Cytosine
C. Guanine
D. Uracil

$125,000

50:50

B or C

$1,000,000

A World Cup qualifying match between what two countries sparked what was known as the "Soccer War" of 1969?

A. Honduras and El Salvador
B. Pakistan and India
C. Uruguay and Paraguay
D. Zimbabwe and Zambia

$250,000

50:50
B or C

$500,000

50:50
C or D

GAME 18

$100

In the James McNeill Whistler painting commonly known as "Whistler's Mother," what is the artist's mother doing?

A. Ironing
B. Cooking
C. Washing
D. Sitting

$200

Submarine, hoagie, grinder and bomber are all names for what type of sandwich?

A. Hero
B. Open-faced
C. Club
D. Wrap

$1,000,000

50:50
A or C

$300

For the first time in over a decade, what band toured with Bruce Springsteen in 1999?

A. The Hooters
B. The E Street Band
C. The Asbury Boys
D. The River Band

A or D

$500

What radio broadcast caused many Americans to believe Martians had landed in New Jersey?

A. "War of the Roses"
B. "War of the Worlds"
C. "War in Space"
D. "War and Peace"

A or C

$1,000

Which of the following is not a statistic required to win baseball's batting Triple Crown?

A. Batting average
B. Stolen bases
C. Home runs
D. RBI's

$300

50:50
B or D

$2,000

Where is the presidential retreat Camp David located?

A. Virginia
B. District of Columbia
C. Maryland
D. West Virginia

$500

50:50
B or C

$4,000

How many horizontal lines make up a standard music staff?

A. 4
B. 5
C. 6
D. 7

$1,000

50:50
B or D

$8,000

For which movie did Paul Newman win an Oscar?

A. *The Color of Money*
B. *The Hustler*
C. *The Sting*
D. *Cool Hand Luke*

$2,000

50:50
A or C

$16,000

By definition, someone who is a quisling is guilty of what crime?

A. Larceny
B. Treason
C. Battery
D. Embezzlement

$4,000

A or B

$32,000

What religious order of the Roman Catholic Church runs Georgetown and Fordham Universities?

A. Benedictines
B. Franciscans
C. Jesuits
D. Dominicans

$8,000

A or B

$64,000

Who was quoted as saying "genius is 1 percent inspiration and 99 percent perspiration"?

A. Albert Einstein
B. Thomas Edison
C. Ben Franklin
D. Yogi Berra

$16,000

50:50
A or B

$125,000

Which media mogul started his career by sending news via carrier pigeon?

$32,000
50:50
A or C

A. Michael Bloomberg
B. Rupert Murdoch
C. Paul Julius Reuter
D. Arthur Ochs Sulzberger

$250,000

Which of the following
substances is used in the process
of making leather?

A. Chalk
B. Sand
C. Granite
D. Salt

$64,000

B or D

$500,000

The 1917 Balfour Declaration gave
British support to what cause?

A. Jewish homeland in
   Palestine

$125,000

B. Yugoslavian unification

C. Colonization of Hong Kong

C or D

D. Home rule in Africa

$1,000,000

What is the name of the tragic clown in Leoncavallo's *I Pagliacci*?

A. Dido
B. Canio
C. Jessonda
D. Rudolfo

$250,000

B or D

$500,000

50:50
A or D

GAME 19

$100

If somebody asks for your "John Hancock," what do they want?

A. Signature
B. Telephone number
C. Impression of John Hancock
D. Firstborn male child

$200

Country star Dolly Parton sings about working what hours in the 1980 song of the same name?

$1,000,000

A. 10 to 6
B. 9 to 5
C. 8 to 4
D. 7 to 3

50:50

A or B

$300

What kind of fruit composed the body of the original advertising creation "Miss Chiquita"?

A. Apple
B. Orange
C. Banana
D. Pineapple

$100

50:50
A or B

$500

What game was invented aboard a yacht by a Canadian couple?

A. Battleship
B. Yahtzee
C. Scrabble
D. Clue

$200

50:50
B or C

GAME NINETEEN ■ 175

$1,000

On what political party's ticket did politician and wrestler Jesse Ventura run for governor of Minnesota in 1998?

A. Democrat
B. Libertarian
C. Reform
D. Republican

50:50
C or D

$2,000

Red Square can be found in which Russian city?

A. Moscow
B. Kiev
C. Minsk
D. St. Petersburg

$500

50:50
A or B

$4,000

With fingers in the standard typing positions, which of these school names can be spelled using the left hand only?

A. Yale
B. Coe
C. Duke
D. Vassar

$1,000

(50:50)

B or C

$8,000

On the television cartoon series, who was Underdog's alter ego?

A. Mr. Peepers
B. Shoeshine Boy
C. Space Ghost
D. Water Boy

$2,000

(50:50)

A or D

$16,000

According to a Hindu legend, from what flower was the god Brahma born?

A. Lotus
B. Hibiscus
C. Carnation
D. Bird of Paradise

$4,000

50:50
B or D

$32,000

In what museum is Michelangelo's "David" displayed?

A. Uffizi
B. Dali
C. Galleria dell'Accademia
D. Louvre

$8,000

50:50
A or B

$64,000

Which of the following has never been an official United States coin?

A. Half cent
B. Large cent
C. Three-cent
D. Half nickel

50:50

A or D

$125,000

Who covered the coronation of Queen Elizabeth II while working for the *Washington Times-Herald*?

50:50

A or C

A. Barbara Walters
B. Jacqueline Bouvier
C. Helen Thomas
D. Audrey Hepburn

$250,000

What modern choreographer had dancers dress in black and slump across stage to jazz music, in the ballet *3 Epitaphs*?

A. Martha Graham
B. Bob Fosse
C. Paul Taylor
D. Mark Morris

$64,000

50:50
B or D

$500,000

What phenomenon allows the human eye to see moving pictures?

A. Persistence of vision
B. Parallax view
C. Photoreception
D. Vanishing point

$125,000

50:50
A or B

$1,000,000

The *Candide* character Pangloss, who claimed that ours is the "best of all worlds," is meant to represent what philosopher?

A. Jean-Jacques Rousseau
B. Gottfried Wilhelm Leibniz
C. John Locke
D. Benedict Spinoza

$250,000

50:50
C or D

$500,000

50:50
A or B

GAME 20

$100

According to the nursery rhyme, which of the following are little boys made of?

A. Snails
B. Birds
C. Worms
D. Flies

$200

What does the "M" in IBM stand for?

A. Machines
B. Manufacturers
C. Malfunction
D. Moolah

B or D

$300

Who of the following was not one of the original *Charlie's Angels?*

A. Sabrina
B. Jill
C. Sara
D. Kelly

$100

50:50
A or C

$500

What former first lady founded a substance-abuse rehabilitation center?

$200

50:50
A or B

A. Betty Ford
B. Patricia Nixon
C. Nancy Reagan
D. Rosalynn Carter

$1,000

According to John Guare's play, how many degrees of separation exist between any two people?

A. Four
B. Six
C. Eight
D. Ten

$2,000

Which of the following is not a color on the standard Twister game mat?

A. Yellow
B. Pink
C. Blue
D. Red

$300

50:50
B or C

$500

50:50
A or B

$4,000

Which jazz musician's nickname was "Bird"?

A. Charlie Parker
B. Thelonious Monk
C. Lester Young
D. John Coltrane

$1,000

50:50
B or C

$8,000

Traditionally, what family of mammals uses a foul-smelling spray as a form of self-defense?

$2,000

50:50
A or B

A. Mustelid
B. Canid
C. Felid
D. Viverrid

$16,000

In the 1984 movie *The Natural,*
what team did Roy Hobbs
play for?

A. New York Yankees
B. New York Mets
C. New York Knights
D. New York Capitals

$4,000

A or D

$32,000

In *The Merchant of Venice,* what
must Antonio turn over to Shylock
if he defaults on his loan?

A. His fiancée
B. 3,000 ducats
C. His entire business
D. A pound of flesh

$8,000

A or D

$64,000

Who was America's first black astronaut?

A. Maj. Guion McNair
B. Maj. Robert H. Lawrence
C. Capt. Frederick Gregory
D. Cpl. Ronald Bluford

$125,000

What U.S. landmark was built on a mudflat known as "Hell's Bottom"?

A. The Lincoln Memorial
B. The Pentagon
C. Independence Hall
D. The Liberty Bell

$250,000

Which of the following is the name of a failed insurrection against British rule staged in Dublin in 1916?

A. Easter Rising
B. Christmas Rebellion
C. New Year's Offensive
D. Halloween Crisis

$64,000

50:50
B or C

$500,000

What author began his career by writing about his experiences as a soldier in the Crimean War?

A. Nikolai Gogol
B. Leo Tolstoy
C. Alexander Pushkin
D. Fyodor Dostoyevsky

$125,000

50:50
A or B

$1,000,000

$250,000

The Electoral College of the United States currently has how many members?

A. 338
B. 438
C. 538
D. 638

$500,000

50:50

B or C

$1,000,000

50:50

B or C

· ANSWERS ·

$100

Game One	B
Game Two	C
Game Three	B
Game Four	B
Game Five	A
Game Six	A
Game Seven	B
Game Eight	C
Game Nine	C
Game Ten	C
Game Eleven	A
Game Twelve	A
Game Thirteen	D
Game Fourteen	C
Game Fifteen	B
Game Sixteen	B
Game Seventeen	B
Game Eighteen	D
Game Nineteen	A
Game Twenty	A

$300

Game One	B
Game Two	D
Game Three	A
Game Four	C
Game Five	C
Game Six	A
Game Seven	A
Game Eight	B
Game Nine	B
Game Ten	A
Game Eleven	B
Game Twelve	A
Game Thirteen	D
Game Fourteen	C
Game Fifteen	D
Game Sixteen	B
Game Seventeen	C
Game Eighteen	B
Game Nineteen	C
Game Twenty	C

$200

Game One	D
Game Two	C
Game Three	B
Game Four	B
Game Five	D
Game Six	B
Game Seven	B
Game Eight	B
Game Nine	C
Game Ten	B
Game Eleven	B
Game Twelve	A
Game Thirteen	B
Game Fourteen	B
Game Fifteen	A
Game Sixteen	B
Game Seventeen	A
Game Eighteen	A
Game Nineteen	B
Game Twenty	A

$500

Game One	A
Game Two	D
Game Three	A
Game Four	C
Game Five	A
Game Six	D
Game Seven	B
Game Eight	B
Game Nine	C
Game Ten	A
Game Eleven	C
Game Twelve	C
Game Thirteen	C
Game Fourteen	A
Game Fifteen	B
Game Sixteen	C
Game Seventeen	A
Game Eighteen	B
Game Nineteen	B
Game Twenty	A

$1,000

Game One . . . . D
Game Two . . . . D
Game Three . . . . B
Game Four . . . . A
Game Five C
Game Six . . . . A
Game Seven . . . . B
Game Eight . . . . A
Game Nine . . . . D
Game Ten C
Game Eleven . . . . B
Game Twelve . . . . D
Game Thirteen . . . . B
Game Fourteen . . . . D
Game Fifteen . . . . B
Game Sixteen . . . . A
Game Seventeen C
Game Eighteen . . . . B
Game Nineteen C
Game Twenty . . . . B

$2,000

Game One C
Game Two . . . . A
Game Three C
Game Four C
Game Five . . . . D
Game Six . . . . D
Game Seven . . . . B
Game Eight . . . . B
Game Nine . . . . A
Game Ten . . . . B
Game Eleven . . . . A
Game Twelve C
Game Thirteen . . . . D
Game Fourteen . . . . B
Game Fifteen . . . . B
Game Sixteen . . . . D
Game Seventeen . . . . B
Game Eighteen C
Game Nineteen . . . . A
Game Twenty . . . . B

$4,000

Game One . . . . A
Game Two . . . . D
Game Three . . . . B
Game Four . . . . A
Game Five . . . . D
Game Six C
Game Seven . . . . B
Game Eight C
Game Nine . . . . A
Game Ten . . . . D
Game Eleven . . . . D
Game Twelve C
Game Thirteen . . . . A
Game Fourteen . . . . D
Game Fifteen C
Game Sixteen . . . . A
Game Seventeen . . . . B
Game Eighteen . . . . B
Game Nineteen . . . . D
Game Twenty . . . . A

$8,000

Game One C
Game Two . . . . B
Game Three . . . . B
Game Four . . . . B
Game Five . . . . B
Game Six . . . . D
Game Seven . . . . B
Game Eight C
Game Nine . . . . B
Game Ten . . . . A
Game Eleven . . . . A
Game Twelve C
Game Thirteen . . . . D
Game Fourteen . . . . D
Game Fifteen . . . . B
Game Sixteen . . . . B
Game Seventeen . . . . D
Game Eighteen . . . . A
Game Nineteen . . . . B
Game Twenty . . . . A

$16,000

Game One . . . . A
Game Two . . . . B
Game Three C
Game Four C
Game Five . . . . D
Game Six . . . . B
Game Seven . . . . A
Game Eight . . . . D
Game Nine . . . . D
Game Ten . . . . D
Game Eleven . . . . B
Game Twelve . . . . A
Game Thirteen . . . . B
Game Fourteen . . . . B
Game Fifteen . . . . B
Game Sixteen . . . . A
Game Seventeen . . . . A
Game Eighteen . . . . B
Game Nineteen . . . . A
Game Twenty C

$32,000

Game One . . . . A
Game Two C
Game Three . . . . B
Game Four . . . . A
Game Five C
Game Six . . . . A
Game Seven C
Game Eight C
Game Nine C
Game Ten C
Game Eleven . . . . A
Game Twelve C
Game Thirteen C
Game Fourteen C
Game Fifteen . . . . B
Game Sixteen . . . . A
Game Seventeen . . . . A
Game Eighteen C
Game Nineteen C
Game Twenty . . . . D

$64,000

Game One . . . . B
Game Two . . . . A
Game Three . . . . B
Game Four . . . . D
Game Five . . . . B
Game Six . . . . B
Game Seven . . . . D
Game Eight . . . . B
Game Nine . . . . A
Game Ten . . . . D
Game Eleven C
Game Twelve . . . . A
Game Thirteen . . . . A
Game Fourteen C
Game Fifteen . . . . B
Game Sixteen . . . . B
Game Seventeen C
Game Eighteen . . . . B
Game Nineteen . . . . D
Game Twenty . . . . B

$125,000

Game One . . . . B
Game Two . . . . B
Game Three . . . . A
Game Four C
Game Five . . . . B
Game Six . . . . D
Game Seven . . . . A
Game Eight . . . . D
Game Nine . . . . A
Game Ten . . . . B
Game Eleven . . . . D
Game Twelve . . . . B
Game Thirteen . . . . B
Game Fourteen . . . . A
Game Fifteen . . . . A
Game Sixteen . . . . B
Game Seventeen . . . . B
Game Eighteen C
Game Nineteen . . . . B
Game Twenty . . . . B

$250,000

Game	Answer
Game One	B
Game Two	A
Game Three	D
Game Four	A
Game Five	D
Game Six	A
Game Seven	A
Game Eight	A
Game Nine	B
Game Ten	A
Game Eleven	D
Game Twelve	B
Game Thirteen	B
Game Fourteen	B
Game Fifteen	B
Game Sixteen	B
Game Seventeen	C
Game Eighteen	D
Game Nineteen	C
Game Twenty	A

$1,000.000

Game	Answer
Game One	A
Game Two	C
Game Three	A
Game Four	A
Game Five	C
Game Six	C
Game Seven	B
Game Eight	D
Game Nine	B
Game Ten	C
Game Eleven	D
Game Twelve	A
Game Thirteen	A
Game Fourteen	C
Game Fifteen	C
Game Sixteen	A
Game Seventeen	A
Game Eighteen	B
Game Nineteen	B
Game Twenty	C

$500,000

Game	Answer
Game One	A
Game Two	C
Game Three	A
Game Four	A
Game Five	A
Game Six	C
Game Seven	B
Game Eight	A
Game Nine	B
Game Ten	A
Game Eleven	A
Game Twelve	B
Game Thirteen	A
Game Fourteen	C
Game Fifteen	C
Game Sixteen	C
Game Seventeen	D
Game Eighteen	A
Game Nineteen	A
Game Twenty	B